THE CLAIMS OFFICE

For Mam and Dad

Dai George
THE CLAIMS OFFICE

SEREN

Seren is the book imprint of
Poetry Wales Press Ltd.
57 Nolton Street, Bridgend, Wales, CF31 3AE
www.serenbooks.com
Facebook: facebook.com/SerenBooks
Twitter: @SerenBooks

The right of Dai George to be identified as
the author of this work has been asserted in accordance
with the Copyright, Designs and Patents Act, 1988.

ISBN: 978-1-78172-090-5
ISBN e-book: 978-1-78172-092-9
ISBN Kindle: 978-1-78172-091-2

A CIP record for this title is available from the British Library.

The publisher acknowledges the financial assistance of the Welsh Books Council.

Cover painting: Kevin Sinnott 'Public Private Life' (detail)
1997 - 2006 Oil on Linen 200 x 208cm

Printed in Bembo by Bell and Bain, Glasgow.

Contents

Reclaiming the View

At her graveside I'm without walls. Safe
from the churn of claim and counterclaim,
I hand myself over to what there is:

six trim mountains overlapping,
the town below, its vest of rain.
I sit on her marble roof and hold

a census of the trees. Here flowerless,
there Nordic in their bristling green;
to her left a spritz of elderflower-white

bubbling off the boughs. Her grave
restores the land to decency. She lived
the life for which I'd fight, but knew

no other way. Eventually the rain
will send me spoiling down the valley
into the fractious theatre of claims

but on her grave top I'm unmanned.
Here there is just the fact of her
bones cuddling under me;

spring lambs the hill over
and, around me, headstones:
their small, laconic messages.

Mergers and Acquisitions

Just as two dandelions choke in the web
                    a spider laid to trick his evening kill,
so do I flail in the net of being born
                    too near technology's final coup.

        At the windiest end of August,
        in a cardigan upon the well-heeled hill,
        I drink with my neighbours – the girl in boots,
        the book swap and the gastro pie – and just

as my kingdom fawns on summer champions,
                    so does a child fasten to a catalogue and cry
methodically in yearning for this toy then that before
                    a rival craze gazumps it and the jilted thing

        goes dusty in a warehouse, boxed.
        I walk back past terraced homes I'll not
        afford in a prism of Sunday springs,
        and just as the pension book signifies

a grizzled sexpot where the taste prefers
                    a salt-and-pepper dusting on the chin,
so in some quarters does my face belong
                    to colour supplements and record books.

        I long to be free of the lurch
        to September with its milksop gifts
        but, just as the river excels in its bed,
        so am I bound to be locked to it.

Just as I rail against the hour that the Web
                    started up its racket in the Logos slums,
so does a weaver take a mallet to his loom
                    and spurn it with a thump to halt the clock.

Nothing alters. This life proceeds
via botched conjunctions, portmanteaux,
through acronyms and bumf. And just as
my death in the eyes of the dying

is but a fissure in a knackered edifice
                    so does my country deserve no song
to mourn its impending eclipse.
                    Yes, this is hostile. This is flowers

        battering like stags to breathe. But
        just as the discovered tomb resolves
        our vision of the Pharaoh's court,
        so may there come a day when gold

clarifies to the flesh it masked. So may
                    our shareholdings melt away and leave
the bullion of our livelihoods: warm bread,
                    purchased homes, and money a neutral liquid.

Poolside at Le Domaine

Brochures would dub those shutters *cornflower blue*
but me, I see a baron plunging out of them, the colour of his blood
pooling on the patio.

You've nipped inside to fix a drink or sleep, while
somewhere close a mower chunters through the noon. Bushes slur
with insects. But I keep the peace,

reclining on a lounger semi-nude
within the *piscine* walls, poster-boy for the new nobility
our parents have secured.

By nightfall we'll be drunk as lords and hatching
desperate schemes of co-authored wealth, the cicadas hammering
distantly away like tills,

but now a bee razors the air along
my ear, and I scare as though caught in the midst of a low
and dirty act.

The handyman feeds the scrapheap. Your mother
sidles through, trilling dinner plans and tidings from Minèrve.
Love, I have to jump

and break the water, the better to hide
these stretch-marks and the suspicion that in me you've made
a bad bargain.

True Eccentrics

As opposed to those who muck about
just outside the bull's-eye.

So none of your neon-smeared
and perfumed chatterers with heads
forever turned to suss their public.

We're talking here of double-twenty freaks.

Garden-shed Edisons buried with their scroll
of blueprints, as though it were a living wife.

King Tubby keeping trim in his lab,
where you check your collie at the door
and everything honks of solder.

Corinthians and vigilantes.

The crested tit, who darts through the pine
on a lunatic prayer, his headdress splayed.

He takes pause in a rotted bole;
halloos forth with tail-feathers
whirring to the Highlands' outer rim.

My Peace, the Ornament

The train squawks its coming with a whistle and the grace
of a rampaging bull swan; it tantrums behind our top-floor flat,
counter-scored below by the witless bus and incontinent van
unloading on the kerb. The gamble is we'll grow used to it,

to noise: its fitful hammers, the minute-by-minute breakage wrought
when the glass bowl that held your peace comes down and freaks
out on impact in a full 360 whirligig. Noise: as much sound's leach
as surge, or the slow dib-dab-dop of that which you most truly hate

becoming horribly liquid, then liquidly real, through the blown tap
that rusts in the dank kitchenette of your former peace. The worst
noise ever came from my ten-year-old throat swelling for the third
time in a minute with soft lowings I could neither explain nor stop.

Ummmm eeeeemmm, it went. *Uuuh eeeeemmm* – fucking up Miss
Mansfield's class. The boys laughed, the girls squirmed. Marked
as mad, I killed the tic. But a siren's blurt can bring me back. A car;
the all-night market with its all-night Arabic commands; the hiss

of docking lorries: they yank me to days when childhood's brain
was a rammed junction, a crossing of trains, and the immaculate,
clockwork timetable of my peace was perverted, pinched, left to rot
in a puddle, as the carriages kept scraping and clanking their brakes.

Metropolis

Your oldest friend leafs a newspaper
in a café, far-off, copying.
He's taken residency for the day,
a monk figuring his manuscript,
pen-nib trembling. Steam mixes
with invading drain smells, burnt coffee,
the paper cranes of tensile thought
as he stitches another character.

Cherry blossom filters to the floor
or snags neon, or doesn't bloom
at all, save for the tourist gardens.
At times, you hanker for spousal rights:
permission to reject the proud,
delicate feats of male friendship
and be with him in Japanese springtime
where he fumbles into new alphabets
and each word is an act of lacework.

Plans with the Unmet Wife

Should we first meet in a market
somewhere equidistant from our lives
and take up the tryst, slightly against choice,

in a city of mutual strangeness;
should lunch hour in a gallery
become a truant afternoon;

should I feel your side and grow privy
to homeland, or the childhood room
where you'd hide and which I'll never visit;

if we have to fly family over
for the ceremony, and tell them straight
that we've altered our bearing,

how is this going to work?
Aflutter from the thought a kid
of mine might be oval-eyed,

I pace Manhattan's narrow rood.
Our dark-skinned and bilingual girl
would be better poised, thank god,

than her old man. Better able to glide
thoughtlessly between her stations,
beholden less to land than tide.

Should people be landlocked, though?
Years from now, you're bathing her
in the sink of our apartment.

Something of the light: your shorter hair
and rolled sleeves have me in mind
of Nan, when she worked a loofah

every Friday against my back.
My parents' weekly respite:
packed off for an overnight,

I remember the peerless heat
of jim-jams from the radiator
sliding over my shampooed head,

and the contours of my second bed –
how Mam was only separate
by twenty minutes of motorway.

Narwhal

Out of a margin which would freeze the lungs
of skimpier and tepid beasts, and all along
her viaducts, her inky play-spots
and her deep canals, she nosed her way
to my imagined shore, till there she was,

a farce: hoar flukes blotched like moss,
camouflage for her liquid copse where sighting
means predation. She breached, as though kiting
with a sack of spuds; gulped, then a fey flop,
oxygenated, back into the deep.

Never trust someone who claims to prefer
animals to humans. You know the type,
some frazzled, cat-kissing petitioner,
whose beaten dogs, like readers' wives,
pout above her stall. Had I any more

reason to love this chubby crybaby –
no sleek kraken or hauling humpback,
no swallower of the wayward – as she
plashed downward, sheathing as though into rock
her eight-foot tooth beneath the waterline,

I may not have blubbered, pointlessly,
nor felt converted by her dopey sport.
I may have missed the slow whitening
of the ocean, or neglected to see
her hung, unfrozen, like a vodka shot.

Hymn to Technique

Tell me who they are, the handsome lads
     tossing a frisbee in a sunny field.
One of them hugs it to his side and hurls
     a perfect centrifugal puck across the day.

Tell me who they are, for to see his friend
     receive and hoick it back is to learn
of a mirror's unerring bounce and to gawp
     at the angular swing of a carpenter's saw.

Now one of them sends a tennis ball so high
     it could bother a kestrel's lofty mooch.
It falls to a stretching hand and – oh – their shirts
     are off, their abs are tanned and brassy-firm.

The type of boys who'd pick a watch's guts
                 for fun and put them back.

That moody kestrel snared, they'd have it hunt
                   a bunny for their pot.

Boys of Leisure

My idylls begin with a turnstile click: a boy

tripping to track his uncle through the Bob Bank gate
          and thence to the stands where he's found a way

to while away his Saturdays with men
          whose muezzin *You are my Cardiff* chants
frightened him so at first but call him now
          irreversibly to the life he needs. Or that

          soft, revolving transfer of force
          that issued when he swiped
          his library card and progressed
          to the Ali Baba glut beyond!

It was the openness of each exchange
and my ordinary faith in how to arrange
a life based on the benefits of now.
I believed that all doors would allow
my passage, though soon enough I came

          to understand the vanity and sudden shame
of hearing that it's over. As a head clunks
          on a cupboard's bottom edge, they erupt in me:
failed vows of stadiums, books and railcards.

          This, then – this might be
          my last pastoral. Come with me;

click through. Imbibe the chip fat vying in the air,
          the chlorine smarting back.
Hasten to the plimsoll squeaks that beckon us beyond
          the pop machines.

In leisure centres we are boys again,

amid retractable nets and banks of bulbs
          whose off-orange glow syrups our cheeks.

You see them best on filthy days,
          on brute November squibs like this: see how
the grey sky coddles on the glass
          like a stranger being welcomed in. Or like us,

          lost and compromised as we are,
          discovering once more the use
          of forsaken thighs and lungs
          in a council-tended baptism.

And the body is grateful, in its querulous way.
It sags on the lip of the pool in cold dismay,
shapeless, white, but turning creamy underwater
as it kicks out and churns the slow lane, tauter,
co-operative again with health's demands.

          It is both a quarrel and a shaking of hands
to swim at once together and stranded
          in the orbits of our thrashing arms
and together still more tragically

          with the baths: great civic fulcrums
          of Hatch End and Pentwyn! Shrines

to a vanishing, turnstile Britain, open to any jack, joke,
          chump who had the change, or no;
to all those who commissioned breezeblocks and tile mosaics
          because the future asked for them.

Referendum on Living

I do well to remember there's a choice.
The world bungles, swarms. For too long I've seen nothing
but breeze rutting in boughs, felt little but this air,
thick with grit and aphids, enter at each orifice.
So much I dislike. Quickly it proves difficult
to resist, an addiction like any other. This week
I've loitered amid bunting, investigated ice
in summer drinks, taken it as proof for fools.
The party spills onto the pavement, repeatedly.

You needn't flaunt skulls in your draughty,
incestuous keep to understand the options
are binary. I sleep in a small room
where orange curtains wad the light.
Elections are dumb sport. Yet still
this intrigue over how to phrase
the question.

The Anecdocrypha

I. Jah

Uncle Andrew, the Pengelli one,
cut the Second Coming's hair.
Summoned from the Kilburn shop
and rustled to an Emperor,

he scoped the ewe's wool on his scalp
and improvised. What he knew
of darkies he knew from his time
minstrelling with polished cheeks

at the Palladium. Still, the trick
was to treat him as you would
any other curly short-arse: to maintain
his natural volume. It was the tip

that clinched it, an imperious fiver
provided so our Andrew knew that,
though His Majesty came in Haile
Selassie, he left highly delighted.

II. Evidence

Blodwen got robbed. The buggers
jimmied the kitchenette window
and cleaned up while she slept
the sleep of the justly retired.

Next day all of Dumfries Street
was baying for a hanging.
Just a week after she leaves
the Dunlop floor for good,

now this. A further theft
was brought to light that evening:
police came round for Blod's
fingerprints, to match against

the windowsill, but her hands
were white flowers, blank
and unencrypted after years
on the Dunlop floor.

III. Balalaika

Now Cyril, now there
was a funny one. Made
instruments – stringed things
mainly – and played them

in a house governed by
the pious, angry whims
of his mam. One Sunday
our self-made troubadour

had a go at 'Ol' Man River'.
His mam had a go right back:
Couldn't you once play a hymn
on the Lord's day, of all days?

Cyril's reply? A shot put launch
to the hearth, where his newest
creation rang out with an open
chord, then broke at the neck.

The George

While most have for their smell the deep
entanglement of beer in nylon underlay,
this joint is scrubbed and temperance-sweet,
at least as far as the far corner where Gran
bequeaths her eternal stash of Lossin Dants.

There's Grandpa strangling the swan who dared
to take a nip at baby Alf, and right behind him
Uncle Alf, lean and in his prime, crooning Haydn
to a brace of pinnied sisters and the highwayman
who someone traced to someone's distaff side.

There's our Huguenot great-grandsire, slopping
in off the Pembrokeshire coast. He pontificates
on the elect, sticks out a hand to feel for rain,
moans his way east to Rhymney, and don't
even get him started on the Treaty of Nantes.

They're all in there, jammed like junked receipts
in a filofax. Beyond them there's the Davies Suite,
and further back the Eveleigh, the Jones: dimly lit,
proliferating function rooms, packed with thatchers
and lay-preaching stiffs, each of them marrying in,

each of them thwacking upon the table his own
lame dowry of myth. Sunday visits. Suicides.
The gypsy someone had a tumble with, and hence
that auntie's Persian eyes. They're all there gossiping
as far as the dark back garden, ignorant of my love.

Claimant

Commoner. Groundling. Outside now with a ticket stub
while your worships feast indoors. Claims you said
you'd see him soon, but worries he'll disturb.
Nose a ruddy bulb. Fidgety and well prepared,

claims his case is due. A waft on him of onions
and dog. Posture patient, but patience as habit, clothes,
as barely noticed burden. Seeks truth and not opinion,
redress before preferment. The man your worships chose

to ignore until this evening. Voter. Yeoman. Entrant
in the world's competition. Knows that openings are near
to nil, but applies in any case. Mistake him for beggar
at your peril. Some will. Some are banking on the sheer

luck of him not fathoming his power. Skin that knows
the weather, soil; eyes that size your privilege.
A brain that spots the subtle, barefaced flaw
in logic that protects you: your pension package

and market share; his debt you were so eager to insure.
Understands the time has come to reassess
his options. That the account's been moved offshore,
the enquiry parked forever in the long grass.

Subscriber. Tenant. And so he remains,
for now at least, scratching his wrists and shuffling
from foot to foot. In robust health. Full corpulence.
Compos mentis and consoled by nothing

so much as the thought of being heard.
Of coming to the fabled endgame in his long,
incremental tramp up from the cattle shed
and Sunday school, rung by dirty rung

up the ladder to your property. Where the feast
continues and his wait prolongs. Where your gate
is shut as he occupies the lawn. Where his ballast
at the base was the condition of your height.

Oran-Bati

1780, give or take: Rotterdam shrugs
into early spring. A tame breeze
riffles in expectant sails and lifts
the dew off cobbles along the quay.

Aboard *De Blijde Boodschap* there's a boy
with achy, reddened ears, a bunged-up nose,
and a clothes trunk that his mother packed
to see him past the Cape.

From here to Indonesia his head
sputters in and out of sleep. He dreams
of saving souls, in a land as warm
as Zeeland in the dog-day months.

When the mission lands, the temperature
defiles him on the spot. A thuggish slab,
as total as the light of Christ, it wets
the last of his home-pressed shirts.

Not for him the bargaining and mosques,
the playful nutmeg scent of the trade routes.
This is vapour, this is groping, this is nowhere
that he knows. Pastoral rounds reveal

the inscrutable rumour of a beast
halfway between monkey and bat:
a mistranslation, he assumes, until
he hears its baby-shriek one night

so dark as to make you lose your way.
His cold has gone. The sniffles of reason
give way to advanced, malarial visions
of a winged creature with womanly curves

and orange fur; an exception that baffles love.
The Word was not written to accommodate
machines, vaccines, the way these days
a note can spirit money overseas,

nor for that matter the simian shape
that lands outside in a pelting rain
and carries a child off in its paws,
a black sail hoisting into the sky.

Different Shoulders

Sleepless again and passing
through the infinite stations
of sleeplessness, I land
for a moment parallel
to the tiny gap between
my pullout and your single bed,
six inches from your mouth.
Our breaths form a cauldron
and I can feel it surfacing,
this dread that I've inherited
the wrong God. That instead
of Christ – so deeply bored
with prohibition that he doodled
on the floor; who'd bless such
happiness and care as we've
found in this, our makeshift
and unmarried bed – we have
the pedant who'd see us burn.

I turn from you, inhale
the pocket of air beyond the bed.
With this shoulder-shift I spin
to a possible world, one in which
I've lived out every day
shaded within abbey walls.
My exemplary life of hops
and alms, where faith grows
in a limpid void and joy
is limbless, where I risk
nothing in my love and all
slows to a platonic lull.

At my back, the kiln of your
breath and your tongue unsticking.
Flesh: its simmering mysteries,
its rogue apocrypha I can't
renounce. I turn a final stage
and fall into our covenant.

Metroland

That part of the world that thrives
  loosely either side of purple-pink
    all the way northwesterly from Baker Street.
      Pure inter-war and after, all roundabouts and Deco sprawl:
        where high-domed malls contend against a perennial 28,000
          sq. ft. of offices to let. Where planes slow at bombing height
            on their way down to Heathrow. Where A-roads
              are redeemed as Views, and still you hear
                a rumble from saloons, the working out
                  of starting salaries and pension plans
                    carried off in tightest harmony
                      between the generations.

Before tertiary services, before the fried chicken drags
  erupted, or the Burtons, being neighbourly, dropped in
    on the long weekend of petals and sweetened milk
      when the Jayakars' girl was married, your mother
        and her family arrived, in rain, and started up
          their negotiation with boilers, in a land where tins
            outflanked bananas on the shelves, and caste
              was *there*, but smaller, a poor option,
                not a barrier to love. They settled here
                  in a land where you got on, got an ISA,
                    kept an eye out for imported crates
                      of Pakistani mangos. They built

a life where, forty decades on,
  I've found a home, an extending house,
    a well-kept place which castled me
      through a winter when the world
        was mess. Its hallway, a cube of light,
          stood as a shoeless, broad reply
            to the grievances that cluttered me,
              the grief that threatened to appear.
                I walked in your garden, drifted
                  centrewards and forsook the clan
                    in favour of your Metroland, where love
                      is a marquee on the newly landscaped lawn.

Bombshell

Lowered down in batches with the corned beef and smokes,
the *Bomba* pin-ups reach the men and pass around the mine.

Their eyes glow, instantly adjusted to the dark that far
from curbing the erratic wave pattern of male desire

has only thickened it to a constant line, a throb that mingles
with other men and dreams of home in the cramped and carnal

dungeon of the mine. Dungeon, yes, but hardly oubliette,
for up there the circus hums, the drills descend: no one could forget

what's happening, least of all the kettled men, whose world at once
shrinks to a span that would hamper a mole and explodes

from knowing of what awaits. Reunion. Parties from here to China.
And now with these *chiquillas* to see them through the remainder,

the mood bubbles. It all seems clear, aside from the puzzle of how,
exactly, to use these *senoritas*. No place for bashfulness while a tough

however-many-weeks are left till light and other halves can end
this screwball noir. They've got this far through being friends,

through organising against the dark. Rotas, then. Taking turns around
the only corner. It works a treat: they finish, splash their hands, return

that little bit lighter to their spots. Except one, who flicks and finds
a blonde in a helmet, her stiletto on a spade. Her smile notices him,

is for him – it says so to the right – and it races up his back
like firedamp, saying they could meet on the other side.

Mojitos

A man who can be kept in mojitos
has very little to worry about.
I chip in five for the shrimp *sofritos*
but you turn me down; tonight's your shout.

In an Upper Westside corner where the food
comes hopelessly before the drinks,
we strategize, give exes attitude
and club together to fathom this jinx:

how is it we can be so wholly free,
so on the brink of going global,
when all our dowdy history
prevents us being here in total?

Good question: mine's another muddled lime,
a glass sprouting mint and spangled with rum.

Tyndale

On panel shows I see them,
in the heat of online arguments,
indignant in the snugs of heritage
pubs, in headshots opposite the agony
aunt beside the going-up-and-going-down
sidebar in Sunday papers: these atheists,
uncombed and open-necked. They
rant about bobbins and fairy tales
and the goals of science and fallacies
they enumerate and link to from online
encyclopaedias. They are quite
funny. They are being retweeted.
They are in the staff room, the tube carriage;
they are patrolling the census figures.
When I think of how there is blood
in their throats when they shout
and of their carping comfort, I tense
for the fight they so dearly want,
but instead of argument

comes the thought of him
hounded to Antwerp, unravelling
the Pentateuch's secret so that soon,
somewhere back in Gloucestershire,
a ploughboy may know God's *Fiat lux*
in the ragged light of his own tongue.

Distraction During Evensong

And they with out taryinge lefte the shyp and their father and folowed hym.
                                                                Matthew 4:22

Hard to say whether it was temperature or memory, birds
garbling through doors as they creaked apart to admit
a late arrival at the back, or a high C that wouldn't merge
with the choral bulk. A marginal sharpness. Something
unappeased, clanging through the semibreve rest, an end
to all the usual comforts.

That afternoon the garden had gushed. The rosemary bush
preened in flower, scented as a wife's closet.
Labour for three hours in the young summer, a wish
granted and granted over with each shear and snip.
A downing of tools. A windfall taken and sprigged in the lamb.
The walk to chapel newly showered.

Now more than tithing was required. An outright auction:
inessentials piled in lots, the life of flannels
and family, ready for the gavel. In place of life, action:
not whipping with birches and salt, but pursuit.
Leave now. Let the dinner burn.

Resuming voice, the choir whined beyond the lectern,
wishful voices winding through the air
like the first snore of a bedmate, a misunderstanding.

Towards the Palatability of Contemporary Faith

Our explicatory Lord is dead.
This week's prayers deduce, or forecast,
a happy God dabbing his hooves
voluntarily in our pastures.

Or God as mild, coexistent moon,
suggestive of our better moments,
not a cranky, jealous child king.
We predict a universal warmth.

Spider woman, raven, the first
burst bladder of sun – all that hokum
set aside, along with the old desire
to blame a harvest on our sins.

As the unattended crannies are swept
and awkward findings brought to light,
our guile increases. Every verdict
can be subsumed and coolly turned

to good effect. We disclaim the cant
of watches found in meadows
and salute our simian forbears.
We cherish proof with the best of them.

Resurrection offered no protection
from a hand that wished to hurt us,
stilled. A shock of love, it still revolts
each Easter from our shrinking crypt.

How the World

Creation, after a time slumming with progress,
reapplied itself on a hillside where my feet
were lizards flirting with the patio heat.

The second day brought a valley of sundried cloth,
towels fluttering a scent of shrubs and myrtle
and afternoon laid flat out, a bronze turtle.

Rain ran its fingertips round the basin's rim,
ushering scowling clouds from the mountain ridge
and a smell of cheese cured three days in a ditch.

Flying ants didn't make it through the night
and lay crusting on a half-diamond marble tile,
all the while life waiting for them to spoil.

The thought of this valley glowing under winter,
with a drift of snow slumbering across the hill,
is how the world became reordered in a lull.

A scorpion came on the final evening
in the muggy funk of a summer downpour,
a jet shard twisting on the glazed tor.

At twenty-five to six, light pushed out the old sky
and coaxed apart the house's stubborn, resting doors
to the basking birds, and cicadas' applause.

New Translation

Thanks to the hacks who still insist
on fixing the smallest glitch in Luke,
the Lord's Prayer can be gamely glossed
at the tenth line. No more is sin a lake
we're led to like bullocks on market-day
but rather rum misadventure:
Save us – and here things get a little coy –
at the time of trial. So censure,
you will note, ceases to be the point.
Our trial will come, with a banal clunk,
certain as a night-time accident
beneath the sheets of a novice monk.
Maybe the poor brother will someday learn
to foil his loins and be reborn

but the rest of us? I have a friend –
how to avoid fogging this with Greek? –
well, *she's seen our photo and seems not to mind.*
By which I mean, I've come into luck,
a jackpot by my normal standard.
Sloping from the corner, she lands
at a Siamese angle by my side,
by which I mean my clammy hands
anticipate her clinch. Am I being clear?
I mean underwear dilates as she roves
into smelling distance, that my pores
seethe with a pheasant reduction, cloves
and other odours of the lavished boy
who can't decide if he wants to try

the wares. I can't, then, but summon my first
speculative shots at courting you,
and your announcement, or perhaps your boast,
I willed against till it proved untrue:
I don't believe in monogamy.

Now, I had to approach a phrase like this
with a certain flexibility,
a feel for the deeper emphasis.
I translated it as a handkerchief
fluttered down to commence the game.
By gradual, doting steps, the bluff
was exposed, we annulled that glum
and altogether too easy vow.
I may have to hold you to it now.

My Accent, the Eunuch

I've watched him from the kitchen,
his fingers running harmlessly across
the garden wall, his wispy moustache
and undeveloped nether regions:
I want to hide him under my stairs,
feed him rice pudding. I've given up
on butcher voices, manly brogues
for shepherding and frying fish.
I've stopped inviting them home.

To remember that time I tried
to sneak in one of my floozies –
a hooligan, or single mother –
and he wrestled them, with all
his dumb, deceptive weight,
to the floor! The love I felt
at that moment was enough.
I don't ask for tall tales, terrace songs,
the society of sots and punsters,

backstory. I don't need a neighbour
by the name of Pat, who visits
weekly to bang on about her soaps
and a do coming up at the Cons Club.
I'd be lying if I said there weren't
times I prayed for him to teeter
and fall neck-down on the other side.
But look at him: those early jowls,
his vague feel of hippo, his eyes
as ugly as they're inoffensive.
He might as well come in.

MMIV

Year of the free period and breakfasting
till just after the post has been. Year of jeans,
buzzing mobiles and *The London Years*.

Eddy Bignose passed his test
and, ever since, the world has puffed
larger, outwards, like a loaf.

Year of stocked fridges and just one year
before we leave. Year of other people's dads
sneaking you in the Fox & Hounds.

Girls grow bored at gatherings
in this year of the lingering video game.
They sit there with their vodka-limes

and wait, like me, for jangling keys,
the Playstation killed and a revving car.
The Gabalfa Flyover is ours.

The Claims Office

Dead centre of the central street
in a town whose principal industries
depend now on the intimate
administrations you can't outsource,
those of tans or care or vinegar.

They pass but scarcely think what's going on.
They assume it starts with an automatic door
and comes to an end, as offices must,
in switchboards, books and obsolescent files
somewhere on the second floor.

But beneath it sprawls a netherworld,
which they'd find if they could only
listen in other ways. If they could
hear the password being mouthed
on a century's worth of wind.

Supposing they could do this,
what might they find below? First, steps.
Ineluctable steps, vanishing behind them
as they made their way through the soil.
A rail that curved towards an open-plan

monstrosity more beautiful than all
the square feet of offices to let
they walk past every day above.
Light the colour of liver disease.
A pummelling, foundry heat.

And, lastly, us: the vaporous,
unstinting clerks whose fate
it is to staff this ruined hall,
this asphodel department where
we find ourselves seconded

long after our deaths, or uselessness,
were sealed in the breathing world.
Our task is simple and without reward.
We sift; we purge; we recommend; we store
our findings in labelled crates. We are

at work to keep the difficult awake:
the intricate, the manual, the lost
or never-realised but hinted-at pursuit
of common spoil and hallowed space.
We maintain the records of our memory,

saving for posterity the string quartet
that packed the Institute, nights in a row;
polio figures in decline and cricket scores;
the order of service at a soldier's funeral
where Lenin was read and then Isaiah.

What else? Yes. We audit. We receive
a copy of every word as it is uttered in
their connected world. Each email chain
and press release. Their action points
and populated spreadsheets. Love songs,

funding reviews, dietary advice:
we collect it all to analyse against
criteria that their pragmatic world
would reject as spendthrift fantasy.
We issue our futile counterclaims:

that one summer soon the lido will be full;
that the burnt heather will grow back gold;
that God is a steel mould into which we pour
molten yearnings, and where the two meet
there rises an inflammable gas.

St Fagan's, for the First and Last Time

The brutalist foyer a relic
from when everyone or, at any rate,
our architects had lost their minds;
water slugging lax through the mill
where the miller's on his one day off
in seven summers; a mother pig
writhing flat-out, dugs-up on the straw,
and you look as though you wish you were
already on the train, fleeing, when
if you can wait, there's a tram.

Honoured guest, I've one more stop
before we leave for home. Nobody
is ever impressed as we hope they'll be
and sure enough your hand in mine
wilts like a leaf on the tannery pool.
I catch myself wanting to thank you,
to make you understand: school trips,
nut brittle, the progress from cottage
to cottage – most of all that I want you
to stay and understand. But we make our way,

in silence, to Oakwood Workmen's Institute,
where we'll close, not with clipboards
and activities (*Year of establishment?*
Subsidies? Where onsite did I once skin
my knee?) but by peering over ropes
to where colliers read Dickens,
followed by my garbled lecture
on betterment – a principle I understand
as much as why tomorrow
I relinquish you to London.

Squander

'I don't care to generalize about this, but I will say that if just one plague-infested rat got ashore from a ship at a New York dock and roamed for only a few hours among our local, uninfected rats, the resulting situation might be, to say the least, quite sinister.'
        from 'The Rats on the Waterfront' by Joseph Mitchell.

I

There were days my breathing came and went
with the ease of a cat in the early hours;
days when hips were glossy divots
and nothing jiggled with my step.
Never a spree that failed to slow
back to a placid, ticking pulse.
Healing happened, and happened
superbly. Blood harboured gentle elves.

A penny span and landed wrong.
Now hips are blotchy, thighs balloon,
I struggle to get two-thirds hard
and lie beside her in a lathering fret
unsure if ever I'll retrieve
the invisible offices of health.

II

Swanning down the gangplank,
already half mad with it and gurning,
he mulls the city with a squint red eye
and buccaneers towards a drain.
Tail slurping through the grate, he splits
to the trench of a subway track
where a native makes a ready friend
to nuzzle through the final days.

Flashpoints. Ferry crossings. The scales
swinging irrevocably out of kilter.
New York boiling through a '50s June. Girls
in Spanish Harlem, frocked and practising
block harmony, who'd gag even to sniff
this tinder to pandemic.

III

Point it out, then, the particular moment
when ingenuity spoiled and our digging,
belching, progress, and breeding went over
to the bad. Whose was the first *emission?*
Prospecting for coal in the hearth,
I dirty my fingers on a dormant nub.
It's ashy, sad, three thousand years apart
from the boon of our inaugural scoop.

Blind and next to blameless, the human rat
divined the problem with his rattiness
at the exact point that his sewer crumbled
and began to overflow. He had it and he
lost it. He scurried beyond the watershed.
He crouched in the rising gunk and slept.

My Ambition, the Rival

He pressgangs me on Saturdays
as I'm sifting through the papers,
when, archduke of my breakfast, I'm
susceptible to my brilliance.

In an autographed gown he sits
to my incredible scrambled eggs.
My perfect coffee snuggles in his palm
while he alleges my potential.

To hear him talk is to promenade
in chinos along a beach speckled
here and there with everyone you've ever
wanted, on a rumoured Riviera.

He thinks I could be huge. He
hates me. His pep talk is a lure
to going absolutely nowhere, because
why would I? While he talks,

I'm already there. I'm the big
poppa. My memoirs are calfskin
and lifetime achievement is a pearly gong
to paperweight my royalties.

His plot against me is to have me
stay with him in eternal breakfast,
where his whisperings may ravish me,
his footsy work up to my balls.

Two Months Left

i.m. Jade Goody

On the day we finally lower our cameras
you'll find me with a ribbon among mountainfolk.
At the instant that her cronies and handlers
slope off, I'll rattle the tin and whoop
then weep, heartlessly in the wild.

A coat-pile overgrows her bed, and
visiting shoes jumble in the hallway,
tripping her as she scuttles by with drinks.
The pall in light may have registered
but you wouldn't know. She extends

the same unreal invite, the same open house
to jackals and well-wishers, only now
there's a curfew. Knowing no other eloquence,
she welcomes, steers, circulates, with all
arrangements in hand for the centrepiece.

Tonight I glorify altitude: pinnacles
where a pyre can burn almost in God's face.
I would kidnap and bathe her waning body
in mountain pools, rest her bald skull
on my lap. There will be no evidence.

Seven Rounds with Bill's Ghost

Those who remember you
as gentle, a point-scorer –
well, they remember you,
I'll give them that.
Oh aye, mild as the wet
of a cat's nose, with a lick
like the rough of its tongue.
Before you got that dicky lung
you could be found, I hear,
exhaling soft advice
through the cherry on your fag.

Propped against the headgear,
I expect, disinclined
to swear or nip behind
for a piss. A good sport, though,
Aye, always laughing
was Bill. Pint-size but useful
in the ring. St John's Ambulance man.
I often think of you as I can:
scarecrowed in an album,
improving, tough to digest,
a bit like bran. Sweeter, mind,

and sometimes linen-shirted,
tanning at a furious rate
in Bournemouth, always with
your son and a vanilla cone,
that grin like a smashed accordion.
Or, much later, convulsed
at every gag in Disney's *Robin Hood*,
oodelallying, while the same son stood
wondering about the time
and if my nappy needed changing
as we both gurgled on the sofa.

Those who remember you,
they've not been backward
in coming forward. Still waxing
about your weave and bob,
your pathological manias
for fair play. So I wonder:
say some chancer pulled a stunt
and it rubbed you wrong – say just the once –
would you ever drop the pipsqueak act
and show him? Say this bloke
might give his wife a little tap.

No sterner lessons
for him, no sneaky
dab of side? I hear you
have to come down hard
and with a twist. Imagine
the parabola, the swoop,
the dash of cranberry as he hits the deck,
the look on the cunt as you wring his neck
and give him something
to slap about. Christian
justice, we could call it.

No, just the lenient jog
to deacon duty, boxing clever,
and clever you were, *Aye,*
never stretched, past the advent
of Tommy Cooper, to the first
and final trip abroad,
when the kinking light on Lake Geneva
dazzled you into a seizure.
Did you not laugh then,
like a creaking outhouse loo?
Or when that last stroke mullered you.

But, Bill, listen,
I'm on Chippy Lane
at chuck-out, and it's all turned
to a gully of garlic sauce.
We've a lad by the smut shop
giving it 'Darling' this
and 'Blue Army' that – some skin slinging
shawarma too close to that poor sod ringing
his girl from a doorway –
and he might be in want
of a word.

Mediation

Heavier than sodden wool, I know the wages
of petulance, how a hairpin can spawn
weaponry. I've lived this crusade as often
as a colonel stranded in foothills, making
sorry progress and executing one man
on each occasion of his private failure.
The holster was my great invention,
my mother tongue a dead language
spoken only in the crevices between
embarrassment and remorse.
So spare me the propitiations,
spare me, both of you, the logic
that would have us trust this as anything
but a cock-up of the first degree.

Chestnut Festivals

Ken heats up milk for proper coffee and slips
three nuggets of baklava on a plate. This man

who taught declensions to the grammar boys of Porth
should know full well that nothing good we do

we do for any reason but itself. We don't
keep Latin half-alive for the edge it lends

our UCAS forms, or to 'connect with the roots
of our mongrel tongue'; we learn it for the loveliness

and pride, the contrarian flair that sees a man
keep a trio of clubs in orbit, or place

a macchiato dab atop his morning cup.
Ken serves Dad and me in the middle room

where once a year we toast the Resurrection
with Campari soda before sitting down

to bitter herbs and lamb. Today, though, we're here
in the name of no cause higher than a jaunt

and so we scarf our pastry and make tracks.
Should be half an hour to Three Cliffs Bay

but ten minutes in we're stuck.
An air show on the Mumbles

has turned the road to car-jammed mush.
Ken rasps a sibilant giggle:

Look at it. Like the Garfagnana,
when everyone clogs the hillsides

to celebrate the latest crop of nuts.
Needless, he means. Like him,

putting the finishing touches on his PhD
a few months shy of turning eighty,

or the party that we're dying to throw
if he'd only let us: our sweet-toothed sage

coiled in the passenger seat and smiling
at bare-chested boys on the beer.

Jakey for the Third Time

I met him on a mountain
dapping up the valley
like a puffin, his every step
admonishment for Christmas
feasts, a coming resolution.
We joked and dawdled
in the wake of his shuttle
past coops and shrines toward
the sky, where he waited for us
and pissed upon the gorse.

This dour little scrumhalf,
thrice my age and fitter –
how could I not reach
for the garland? Twice since
I've tried to capture him
and, twice repelled, I've lost
his stoop against the mountain
and our banter, flasks, the fresh
of winter. This useless
fetish for older men!

A Clifton Postcode

Of course, we lived with perpetual damp
and hypochondria, refurbishments,
in run-down mansions where the very stone
was tainted dimly by the sugar trade.
Which explains why ackee stewed on hobs
in markets we fled to on odd weekends
when hangovers had given out to sun
and we announced ourselves among the chic,
the latte-breathed, pushers of tricycles,
all those who kept to their Fridays' plans.
Days we would take our place in St Nick's yard
with families flowered between the stalls,
the two of us cradling trays of the stuff,
this fishy gloop we'd decided to like
and then did like, and then completely wolfed
down to the yellowed polystyrene box.

Though I wish it still, I shouldn't hint
we lived as one; not strictly or without
a grudge. True, though, that I came to you
on daily rounds, at such hours that I half
expected milkmen, even mourned their late
and unaccounted absence from your street,
which stood just on the desirable side
of Whiteladies. Out of your door and left,
the road bucked, then flattened, then swung around
on its obsequious course past the Downs,
those simpering shops of artisan cheese
and pre-electric kettles. You'd be fast
asleep by the time I was on my way,
dragging myself the half-mile east to home
through yummy mummies and their steel-frame prams,
my mouth watering for salt fish and jerk.

Inside the Company

My mole meets me behind tubs of municipal
                    azaleas, hidden from the five-abreast
Friday lunch-hour foot traffic with my visitor's
                    pass sweated to scraps in his hand.

He is tight-lipped, harassed, a security-pro-
                    cum–cleaning-operative-cum-refreshment-
trolley-pushing-everyman, ancillary service
                    made flesh, in visible turmoil over

the imminent fact of his beautiful defection.
                    But I have my ways and know to use
the imminent, beautiful and, for the last time,
                    visible contours of the company HQ

to win him back around. Look at it, I say.
                    Drink it in. This architecture uniquely fit
for heroism at long last overrides the girder-
                    like compliance drummed into him

by the dead hand of his original welcome
                    pack. Smoked glass and bludgeoning
height, the sense that walls are windows
                    in service to curvature, that the building

is a waterfall: it wins him back around.
                    A last inspirational pep talk and I'm in.
I take his pass, which laminates in my
                    hand, and saunter past reception.

Where next? A pressing question. It's
                    minutes till Singapore markets close
and I'm hell-bent on seeing this happen.
                    I want to see the sorcery, the jazz,

the glass at the moment of being smoked:
                    I want to see unholy amounts of money
spurt through the eye of this needle-fine
                    transaction. I want to catch them at it

but all I get is carpeted luxury-hotel interior
                              and a lift that presents options so vast
I get *à la carte* anxiety. Sixteenth floor:
                              whatever. I bing the button and I'm in.

Doors open to sunset's apricot siege
                              on the building's east-wing window-wall,
a ridiculous, a very near Nirvanic assault
                              on my recalcitrant concern for forwards

and futures, my eye on the methods that sped us
                              here, and are poised to do so again.
Not caring feels better. I relax into money's
                              beatific colour scheme, imagine myself

a part of this, a player – but there he is, my mole,
                              going *pssst* behind the potted palms.
He points to a trolley, and I don't mean of the sandwich
                              kind. It's loaded to the teeth

with instruments of unparalleled connection:
                              instruments for flogging derivative
instruments; computers that can link
                              Chicago up to SGX in less than a fraction

of the time it takes to break a sweat,
                              or hope. I think this might be it; I try
the door and I'm in. Through a jungle of cables and power-
                              points aglow, shrunk to a fraction

of my original size, I peer down the barrel
                              of a USB port, breathe deeply as it
breathes me in. Surfacing on the hard drive's manic
                              grid, I rush towards a tiny room, and this

is it: I am in the algorithm, bouncing like
                              a basketball, and only now, with figures
swarming as I try to scream, do I reach for the
                              nail-bomb strapped against my chest.

Prospectus

Our pretties, our soon-to-be potentates,
to let you through these ivy-wrangled gates
we need to see you grasp a simple truth,
of which your suppers might supply the proof:
namely, that the perfect, useless syllogism –
though picked apart and parsed, a prism
of endless reflecting necessity –
resembles nothing, in its QED,
so much as the perfect Dundee cake,
the sort a wry and handsome girl might bake
after quiet years following an aunt.
We'll taste the soundness in your argument
like gouty connoisseurs, apt to discern
a caramelized almond from one burned,
but, rolling the liberal counterpoise
of sultanas, zest and – fortunate boys! –
a glob of scotch, might equally decree
your offering uncommon. Then, jubilee
as we divvy it into paper towels,
and through sweetened mouthfuls make avowals.

Queen's Lane Approximately

Pass along it, a byway curved against
    the college backsides,
        long and looped as a novelty straw and not
belonging to you, as skiing couldn't,
    or an easy answer
        to the question on everyone's lips these days
about what you've been doing
    since you were in a place
        not altogether different from this.

Under a bridge no higher
    than a lanky uncle, you dodge
        a gush of bicycles, making way yet managing
somehow to do it wrong, to cut them off
    at the next bend. You are pilgrim here, a guest,
        and you worry they can catch the scent
of sweat pricking in your armpits
    too early in the day.
        So however much you're able to assume

hauteur about the mixed-metaphor
    period effect (gas lamps
        dangling by portcullises; the round,
washed-out parsonage window) you creep and stare,
    neither free to join the fag-break cooks
        in the gravy smells wafting out
of St Edmund's pedigree arse, nor pedal
    alongside the scholars, out into the wide,
        golden plateau of Broad Street

        where the town is languidly revolving
        about its business like a girl called Jane;
        where they've sent back all your invitations
        and they won't be seeing you again.

New York on a Shoestring

for Andrew Jamison

Forget the Highline, AJ, this
is how to see the place as locals do.
Catch the L from an outer Brooklyn stop
where the street view spans a block or two
of Puerto Rican flags and packed-out stoops,
and watch as the carriage doors admit
successively more besuited cargos.
Soon a PA's daubing lippie standing up,
while a tieless Wall Street brat gives up his seat
to a pregnant hipster, whose studded bra shows
from underneath her ripped Dead Kennedys top.
They all wriggle on and off the shared chrysalis
that is the train, on which you play no less a part
in some other tourist's perfect NYC tableau.
At Union Sq, the frat boys come and go,
bulling about beer pong and René Descartes.

Next stop: the immaculate PA departs
and starts the perfect walk I have for you.
Follow her to the uptown interchange
or make for daylight on 6th Avenue
but, either way, first revel in the lunge
of sixty bodies through the underpass.
This bit the guidebooks fail to mention,
and even if they did they'd only whinge
about the sharp odours of shit and saturated fats
at whose rampant and unholy, daily emanation
our PA retches, willing it just this once to change
through the power alone of two judicious squirts
of Davidoff Cool Water. A Guadalajaran janitor
running late beside her smells the shit smell too,
her cucumbery scent, and before she's out of view
clocks her nose crinkle on a CCTV monitor.

What he makes of that I won't presume,
whether or not he thinks, *Hey bitch,*
it's my city as well, and your stink.
For, AJ, the island here is rich
and complex in its enterprise and junk,
and the people who seek it won't conspire
with our motives for them being there.
We have the city and our dream for it. We think
we're owed its thrumming nights and happy hours –
either that, or we're owed the plane fare.
But these two know where their own dreams rank
in the city's impossibilities. So track her perfume,
as she ducks and sprints to catch an uptown 1,
or watch him as he crests on W14th Street.
Only, you have to want this. You have to barrel out
and barge your way through the columns of sun.

Reclaiming Terra Firma

Above the weather, in the dark,
I'm travelling home to spite the ocean.
You're sleeping leagues below and east

or trying to, I'd hope, as I am,
huddled in the window. I peel
the blind and see the fruit of being

hitched to the turning world: dawn
gained ahead of time, a mauve horizon
seeping light, halfway over Greenland.

What two years were these? Clouds
foam around the engines and the air,
lucent now, though thickening,

rocks me to my seatbelt. Two years
of leaving off and broaching; feast weeks
when we met and ate to honour bodies

then fallow months between.
Well it's over now. The plane dips
and all the arguments we're yet to have

rear up from the ocean, this ocean
of two years' obstacle, which kept us
in two years' tenderness and infancy.

Could you possibly be sleeping now?
Life-size homes and lakes appear
and with them, ever larger, our paradigm

for future years: a white morning; a terminal
steadying into work, where soon we'll kiss,
as the ground hunches its back to meet us.

Acknowledgements

I am grateful to the following journals and anthologies, where some of this collection's poems first appeared, occasionally in slightly different versions: *Bird Book* (Sidekick Books); *Boston Review; Clinic II; New Welsh Review; Oxford Poetry; Poetry Review; Poetry Wales; Pomegranate; The Salt Book of Younger Poets* (Salt); and *Transom.* 'Poolside at Le Domaine' featured in *Best British Poetry 2011* (Salt) and 'Seven Rounds with Bill's Ghost' appeared in the 2013 instalment of the series.

The older poems in the collection were written while I completed an MFA at Columbia University and first appeared in my thesis. Thanks are due to my teachers, Lucie Brock-Broido, Josh Bell, Timothy Donnelly, Sarah Manguso and Nick Laird, and to the St David's Society of New York, who made my study at Columbia possible through generous financial assistance.

Several poems grew out of themed readings hosted by Roddy Lumsden at the Betsey Trotwood. 'Oran-Bati' was my contribution to a crypto-zoology project and 'The George' to a surname project. 'Inside the Company' is the result of an evening called Opposites Attract, where I collaborated with Sophie Collins on the theme of public/private. I am grateful to Roddy for inviting me to take part in these events, and indeed for all of the encouragement and advice he has given me over recent years. Many of the poems in this collection have benefited from the input of Roddy's Wednesday group.

Finally, I thank my family. Whether their surnames are George, Davies, McKelvay or Keeble, they have all provided moral and material support beyond compare, and this book is dedicated to them with love.